Business Secrets for Corporate People

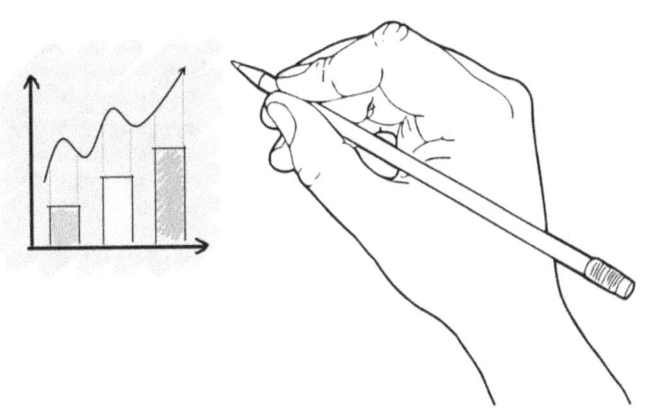

MSK Muhaiyuddin

Copyright © 2020 MSK Muhaiyuddin

All rights reserved.

ISBN: 9798558886016

DEDICATION

I dedicated this book to the universal intelligence and those who really seeking the guidance to start or re-start life Journey with intellectual happy.
Life is nothing but result of mind function and process, mind is nothing but Knowledge - MSK Theory
This book will completely reveal the secrets of success for corporate people.
This is our universal contribution and dedication to the all souls to live life with continuous happy.
Also my soul full gratitude my beloved best friend profession Dr Krthic.K.yen & Sathiya
MSK Executive Ifperiya Madam. Associative psychologist MSKM.Mubusshereena with all our blessing soul and universal intelligence who this opportunity to serve.

With soul gratitude
MSK Muhiyuddin CEO & Corporate psychologist
MSK Life clinic Foundation

CONTENTS

	Introduction	i
1	Corporate View	Pg 2
2	Business Branding Skill	Pg 6
3	Human Capital Development for Industries	Pg 9
4	Top 50 Therapeutic Components in MSK Industrial Development	Pg 14
5	Top 20 Business Theories from Mind Set Knowledge Psychology	Pg 19
6	Top 10 Cash Balance Rules From Mind Set Knowledge Psychology	Pg 23
7	Top 5 Money Earning Rules From Mind Set Knowledge Psychology	Pg 26
8	The Major Difference Between Rich and Poor Mind Set	Pg 29
9	The Secrets of Success of Corporate People	Pg 32
10	Who is Professional Consultants for business	Pg 36

INTRODUCTION

Petrol is useless if you do not know how to drive a vehicle. Similarly, if you start with money, a business will not happen automatically.

You can drive a vehicle if you know how to operate. But to be a good driver, you need to know the various nuances of operating vehicles on the road beyond that. There are various subtleties to business as well!

What are their nuances?
Some people say that experience is the basis for doing business.
If a business requires experience, why don't all the older people who do business become rich?

Some people say they can do business if they have the money. So why are all the bank owners giving money without doing business?

Suppose a business is a process to inflate profits by pouring in debt without updating the industry's operations to keep pace with the changing times and needs. What is the name for the process of maximizing profits by using intelligent people in every action to meet the needs of changing people and grow their company?

If a business is to run well, it is unlikely that it will be profitable to do business with what we know without having a clear idea of what it requires! Only those who realize what business need become corporate bosses. The purpose of this book is to reveal that secret!

BUSINESS SECRETS FOR CORPORATE PEOPLE

In this book, the following things are explained clearly and concisely in a way that is easy for everyone to understand!

Doing business with money is the second stage of doing business! So the first level......?

To what extent does business experience contribute to business growth?

Can I borrow and do business?

What activities should you do if you are starting a business?

What is 'corporate'? What is the secret of their success?

How do we deal with those who become competitors for our business?

What to do if you know your business is heading for failure?

What is Business Branding Skill? How can you develop that skill?

What are the primary obstacles in Human Capital Development for Industries?

Top 50 therapeutic components in industrial development psychology

Top 20 business theories from mindset knowledge

Top 10 cash balance rules from mindset knowledge

Top 5 money earning rules from mindset knowledge

The significant difference between the rich and poor mindset

With whom can you ask for advice on our business development? With whom should I not ask? How to deal with the different moods that plague those who want to make money? The answers to various questions still unknown to professionals are given very clearly and concisely in this book! Not only this, but if you have any doubts about this after reading this book, the phone number and address you should contact given at the end of this book!

1. CORPORATE VIEW

Even if you see a hungry lion as a lion, that lion will see you as food! Similarly, there is a lot of difference between the way you look at your life, money, career, debt, failure, success, etc. and how corporate people look at the same things! It is their vision of success that makes them winners!

We have explained a successful vision here through MSK (Mind Set Knowledge) Business Theory! Understand this, and you can easily understand the secret of the success behind the successful corporate bosses!

1.1 An overview of a business!

Suppose a person starts a business at the age of 25. Then there would have been a demand for his product. People would have bought his item because of that demand. He is doing business, thinking that he needs money and experience for business!

But over the day, many people will see that he is doing business, and they will start a similar business, thinking that it will go well! Now it comes to the saturation point of his business!

There is an updation that is for business! If this type of update is not doing in terms of quality and product, it will not be able to fight together with time! This concept is not understandable to ordinary people!

But corporate people know their business in 3 stages of what is happening, what will happen, what is happened! According to them, business is not a repeated act of buying and selling!

It is a behavior pattern that encompasses the various functions that people, their activities, and technology form in a combination of these three!

If you start with money, the business will not happen by itself! If you do not know how to drive a vehicle, petrol is useless! The company has the same psychology as driving! This concept is only visible to the naked eye!

1.2 Overview of money!

We think we can do more business if we have the money! If this is true, then not all bank holders need to be paying; they can keep their money and run the business themselves. You can not build a business with just money. If you develop a business, the money will come automatically.

Doing business with money is the second step! The first step is to make money by working hard and investing in the equipment needed for that work! This fact is known only to the corporate eye!

1.3 Overview of Business Experience!

We think business needs more experience! If we look at the many people who have failed in business today, they would have just started that business without any occasion when they started it! But there would have been a lot of experience when it failed. Yet their business would have died! So, if the company grows by experience, then all the older people in the world today must have been rich! So your experience may increase as you age, but attitudes in your business will not grow. Business needs intelligence, not only knowledge! This fact is also only known by the corporate eyes!

1.4 Overview of Debt!

We think borrowing can grow the business. But credit must be the amount of prey needed to catch fish! If you catch prey to a fish's size, you will have to rescue the fisherman from the fish itself! This fact is also understandable only by corporate people.

1.5 Overview of industry competition!

If a man says, "I have competitors," corporate people will not agree with him! Because every human being, every second, is different in knowledge, skill, and experience from others in every way! So there is no one rival in the world!

1.6 Overview of failure!

If we find that our business is failing, we may be confused about whether this will happen or not, and start looking for something else! But the career is the child we have! Or the parent who loves us! Can these two be replaced?

The thought of leaving your business as the child you have raised for about 20 years or your career as the parent who has raised you for 20 years should not just come to mind! If so, that means the problem is with technology, not with the industry!

Then we need to change technology, not business.

As far as corporate people are concerned, they will never come up with the idea of seeing anything other than this except to see how they can perform better than others from what they are now!

https://msklifeclinic.in/business/

2. BUSINESS BRANDING SKILL

What personal development in you will multiply your business? The answer is the Brand Building! As an entrepreneur, most of us try to solve an existing marketing issue or a gap monetized to create a massive business proposition. Business branding skills will provide the solution for all your problems.

Most of the entrepreneurs strive to solve a current marketing problem or a gap that may monetize to make a massive business proposal. Business Branding Skill will solve their problem by minding their Branding, brand affinity technology, brand ambassador, brand avatar, brand recognition, brand extension, brand goose, brand identity, brand image, and brand iron.

2.1 Brand Equity

Brand equity is the industrial value that derives from customer perception of their brand name of a specific product or service, rather than in the product or service itself. It is a phrase used in the advertising business which clarifies the value of having a well-known brand name, depending on the idea that the owner of a renowned brand name can create more.

Brand Equity is the value of a product satisfying customers' expectations over other goods. Your brand's equity is significant since, if your brand has positive brand equity, it is possible to charge more for your products and services than the generic products or alternative competitors.

2.2 Why brand equity is vital?

Brand equity identifies a value premium a company creates from a product with a recognizable name compared to some generic equivalent. Companies can create brand equity for their products by making them memorable, easily identifiable, and exceptional in quality and reliability.

2.3 How is brand equity calculated?

It believes the valuation of future net earnings may be attributed directly to the manufacturer to determine their brand's value in its current usage. This technique's brand value is equal to the present value of income, cash flows, or cost savings actually or hypothetically due to the asset.

2.4 The difference between brand value and brand equity

Brand equity and new value are measures that estimate just how much a brand is worth. The difference between the two is that brand value refers to the monetary advantage that the business records on its balance sheet. In contrast, brand equity refers to the importance of the new to a customer of the company.

2.5 How do we handle brand equity?

To handle brand equity, you need to manage the brand picture during a lengthy period. This work entails keeping the same brand promise you've made to present customers or the newest guarantee you're likely to drive into the brand new clients. For top brands, the brand image is all.

https://msklifeclinic.in/industrial-development/

3. HUMAN CAPITAL DEVELOPMENT FOR INDUSTRIES

Only machine quality could be keep managed & developed occasionally in all aspects. Now the questions are;

- What about the quality care of guys?
- Just how will it maintain?
- What factors to considered in this upkeep?
- When should it be kept?
- By whom it ought to hold?

3.1 The Primary Obstacle in Human Capital Development in Industries

Every human being has a distinctive mindset; just a couple have a winning attitude. Others possess the Mind Establish that loses their lifetime unconsciously and their belonging (it might be private, industry, and establishment). Within our practical performance based study, most folks from the era of Six to Sixty working in their subconscious mindset that's irrelevant to the correct real organizational (or) intuitions goal to their personal aim.

3.2 The significant defect in industrial developing syllabuses for human capital maintenance

These days, product quality has maintained the same materials & scientific updated knowledge. But, still up to this outbreak age, for individual capital upkeep, all industries are unconsciously and consciously following PowerPoint-based syllabus, together with amusement game by entertainment training & trainers.
The majority of the organization (or) intuitions are after the traditional way of Human Capital Development. This method will enter their Ear & Eye

with enjoyment mode, but maybe not enters to their Mind for permanent execution level.

Human capital's quality output signal has to derive through an exact human upgraded individual emotional process.

3.3 The traditional training system and its difficulties

For Industrial Development, in the standard training method, players are requested to tick feedback form about the training content and coach participation at the close of the syllabus training.

Just presume, patients are requested to tick the comments form with the identical industry like questions. Some example queries are;

Your view about the doctor's surgical operation

Have you been like this therapy?

How the surgical procedures fitted to you

Give a quality mark to the doctor's operation.

Can this surgery or treatment alternatives to your physic and family

Are you currently satisfied with medication, prescription by doctors-give your regular

Are you currently interested in his treatment?

Are they flowing correct medical processes?

These are some examples of industrial feedback replicated in patients around physicians. Some industrial direction individuals are still can't realize the inner meaning of this 'ours' concept fact about the legal opinions system. Instead of understanding, they argue to withstand their traditional feedback system. But reality never fails.

3.4 Some Big Questions to realize the ineffectiveness of classical training methods

Some concerns (called MSK Big Q's) are given here for realizing the ineffectiveness of the classical training methods.

BUSINESS SECRETS FOR CORPORATE PEOPLE

MSK Big Q -- Number.1:

How do patients assess the physician's medical procedures & process?

MSK Big Q -- Number.2:

Is it possible to repair and improve the performance of machine other mechanisms?

MSK Big Q -- Number.3:

Is it possible to do surgery by a very long experienced social person?

MSK Big Q -- Number.4:

What's the difference between Training and Therapy?

MSK Big Q -- Number.5:

It's possible; Trainer can alter the internal psychological pattern of their industrial staff or industrial workers?

If it's possible means may ably to treat behavioural issues of people.

MSK Big Q -- Number.6:

Is it possible to modify the personal ability and inner understanding by training?

MSK Big Q -- Number.7:

Is it possible, without alteration, all machines will function for industrial needs?

MSK Big Q -- Number.8:

Is it possible to repair different machines from precisely the same mechanics?

MSK Big Q -- Number.9:

Can it be possible to carry out the same surgery on all folks?

MSK Big Q -- Number.10:

Can you (game at the training session) entrainment enhance productivity?

MSK Big Q -- Number.11:

Is it possible the same qualified applicants are the same psychological quality?

All these would be the MSK Big-Q's to realize the fact for Industrial Development.

Human intelligence means mental quality that consists of their skills to learn from experiments. In other words, experience adapts to new situations, understand and manage abstract theories, and use knowledge to control one's environment, including the ability to recognize patterns, strategy, innovate, solve problems, make decisions, keep the information, and use language to convey. Human intelligence is predicated on the variants the social encounter in life and reactions on account of functions and procedures total in their lives. So analyses of various therapeutic components are essential in industrial development.

https://msklifeclinic.in/international-learning/

4. TOP 50 THERAPEUTIC COMPONENTS IN MSK INDUSTRIAL DEVELOPMENT PSYCHOLOGY

1. Industrial and Intuition Policy Evaluation
2. Organization Behaviour Evaluation
3. Work or Service Productivity and Development Analysis
4. Work Qualifications and Working Attitude observational-based analysis
5. Quality of Work-Life
6. Performance and Human Error Analysis
7. Psycho-Physic Health Evaluation and Human Relationship Analysis
8. Individual Communication Barrier-Analysis & Effective Communication with Co-workers
9. Top to Bottom Co-ordination & Co-operation Analysis
10. Worker Engagement Analysis with Happiness & Productivity
11. Organizational Culture Defining & Work-Life Balance Evaluation
12. Hierarchical dynamics & Optimize Workplace and Processes
13. Industrial Well-being Development
14. Industrial Cognitive Re-Structuring for Management & Staff

15. Staff & Workers whole family analysis including child behaviour and education

16. Industrial Battle analysis and de-conflicting

17. Industrial and Societal stress Investigation and Immunology

18. Industrial Ergonomic and Health Issues Evaluation

19. Emotional well-being analysis. This component includes dispositional optimism, hypertension, and diabetes Stress and Melancholy, comorbidity and coping strategies.

20. Personal and industrial coping strategies & problems of everyday life analysis

21. Industrial demands and conclusion deriving evaluation - maximizing potential utilization

22. Industrial Fatigue and sleep deprivation analysis and treatment

23. Private de-addiction including digital, mobiles, TV, substance

24. Fatigue and sleep deprivation, smoking habit

25. Competing responsibilities at work and home

26. Self-management & collaborative direction

27. ADHD symptoms at work, manifest as disorganization, failure to meet deadlines, inability to handle workloads, problems following directions from managers, and arguments with co-workers.

28. Problem-Solving and working skills

29. Goal setting & goal achievement process

30. Corporate social responsibility

31. Corporate learning -- globalization, coping with more significant rivalry

32. Occupational health, improving interactive affirmation processes with security and well-being

33. Leadership Training- Work motivation and approaches -tactical change.

34. Trust Building. Trust is vital to teamwork, and it starts with people knowing each other mutually with staff Transparency.

35. Analysis for greater absenteeism, reduced production, resolving massive customer complaints on products and services.

36. Work variables analysis including, time stress, hectic work, and more accountability, monotonous work, shift work, work under the threat, psychological anxiety, responsibility and workforce associated sleep disturbances, burn-out syndromes and depression.

37. Industrial People participative management evaluation. This component including rigid regulations and rules, Restriction on behaviour, lagging of participation in the decision-making process, lagging of effective communication, psychological distress, lowered self-esteem and job dissatisfaction anxiety variables.

38. Industrial subjective skill. This component includes productivity evaluation for well-being. This component comprises such as perceived self-efficacy, autonomy its range, lagging of competence and recognition of potential ability, un-realizing intellectual capacity.

39. Confidence Building, Confidence, action analysis & Team management. Improving attitudes toward authority and hierarchy

40. Therapeutic Time Managements (Time management and mind direction)

41. Intra -- Interpersonal Relationships advancement & Management. Reducing gaps in understanding and perspective, Lack of focus, attention, distractions, or irrelevance to the recipient, passive listening.

42. Supervisory Qualities/EQ/SQ/IQ/superior or inferior skill complex

43. Stress Management & balanced life Direction

44. Work anxiety analysis- Tension/ Indecisiveness/Emotional problems/anxiety/work errors / lack of Initiative Taking Ability/ Restlessness/anger/frequently damaging things

45. Employee Assistance Programs (EAP)

46. Industrial wellness Tourism with outbound learning

47. Industrial lifestyle direction and Human capital optimization

48. Industrial work system & Office work system designing and growing

49. Learning curve development & alteration

50. Store management - external & internal supply chain management

https://msklifeclinic.in/corporate-presentation/

5. TOP 20 BUSINESS THEORIES FROM MIND SET KNOWLEDGE PSYCHOLOGY

1. Business is what people do is the repeated act of buying and selling! But it is a Long Term Process that includes a unique system with planning and auditing systems they can execute it with size! It is only visible to the corporate eye.

2. Technology alone is not enough for your business success! Speech technique is also required. The value of smart work can be calculated with a pen! But without work, it is useless.

3. The only personal skill that managing directors have is the knowledge to use intellectuals! Ordinary people do not seek advice using brains in the mindset that they know everything for themselves.

4. How money works depends on how his mind works and operates. Rather than worrying about money, plan to know how to make money.

5. How to get money is different! How to make money is different.

6. Every object has a dynamic nature. There is also the nature of directing that object. The entrepreneur who can run the business must be familiar with that movement.

7. A business will not happen if you start with money! Petrol is useless if you do not know how to drive a vehicle. The company has the same psychology as going.

8. Business is a combination of people, their activities and technology.

9. Business intelligence is a process that starts with data integration, collects information and makes it Intelligent until Decision Making.

10. Wealth is not money. Good mind. Business needs it more than money.

11. KARMA is not a religious doctrine. According to MSK Theory, KARMA stands for Knowledge Analysis Reorganizing and Mind Acceleration. One can get rid of karma if approached scientifically.

12. Rotating law for love and money is same! Grow if given! Refuses to come if you refuse to give

13. Avoid working and try to get money directly is a modern begging.

14. Today tutorial education that makes you believe that you need money to do business! But only corporate owners understand the need for business acumen to do business.

15. The boss only cares about the job more than he cares about the employee. The worker tends the employer more than employment. This mentality is understood by the worker over the age of 40. Some do not realise for life!

16. Money comes from human energy. This understanding requires the ability of the mind to operate the machine of labour—no need for magic.

17. Tutorial education is not required for Physics, Chemistry, and Mathematics to rule the country. Human psychology is just what is needed.

18. If you are looking for lending companies, it means that the lender is looking for you. You can not borrow and become a boss. But the loss will wait for you.

19. Corporate Counselling isn't just dealing with business problems. It can also be a tremendous life tool for achieving personal growth and happiness with wealth.

20. What is happening now is that the shoddy work and become rich, and the children of the rich become poor without working. This happening is a kind of psychological cycle.

https://msklifeclinic.in/msk-corporate-professionals-listening-skill/

6. TOP 10 CASH BALANCE RULES FROM MIND SET KNOWLEDGE PSYCHOLOGY

1. Love money. Be happy to say that you got a decent pay for the work. Do not torture and collect the money that someone else has to give.

2. Do not fake money by saying that you got so much. Do not be greedy for money.

3. Happy to give back the money purchased. Don't spend money on pride.

4. Money is not available through prayer. You only get paid if you work.

5. Save money. Only small savings will later become immovable property.

6. Don't spend money plentifully when you have money. Do not be stingy in the name of saving money. Do not save money by grieving yourself.

7. Money should not be kept anywhere. It should be placed in the appropriate place.

8. The money that came in regularly is the rest to go to expenses. Do not waste money, saying that money will be coming if you give.

9. Do not grieve yourself, thinking that you can be happy if you have a lot of money.

10. The money will take you to the tower. Understand that at the same time, it makes you stand outside the same building!

https://msklifeclinic.in/corporate-decision-making/

7. TOP 5 MONEY EARNING RULES FROM MIND SET KNOWLEDGE PSYCHOLOGY

Do you want to earn more money and join the rest? If so, you should follow the MSK Money Collection Rule.

Rule No-1:

In your savings, make sure that the amount saved is ten thousand to go towards expenses with the help of your labour. If not, start saving from today!

Rule No. 2:

Try to increase the savings from 10 thousand to 50 thousand.

Rule No. 3:

Sleep to work to turn fifty thousand into a million. Your hard work should not affect anyone's mind. Don't involve anyone's money. The only thing left to do is to save the rest of the money for family members to do their duty generously and happily without wastage.

Rule No. 4:

Save up to one lakh, one and a half lakh, 2 lakh, up to 10 lakh.

If you approach credit counsellors and think effectively about the tactics of getting money from them

Or if your family advises you not to live in this world without borrowing and acts accordingly, the money will turn into a loan instead of savings for you! That means little happiness will create more monetary loss.

Rule No. 5:

Find out if your money is in a savings account or a credit account. The reality is that you are living a debt-free life if the deficit is only 10%. 90% debt means that you are deceiving yourself, selling your health, losing your mental health and lowering your social outlook.

https://msklifeclinic.in/corporate-argument/

8. THE MAJOR DIFFERENCE BETWEEN RICH AND POOR MIND SET

The activity of the poor and the activity of the workers are both only towards money. They do not want to take technical and business advice for advancement from qualified professionals.

They believe that only the level of knowledge they know is inevitable. They want to borrow more. But do not want to borrow knowledge. The result is that they live only as workers. Their lives are going somewhere under the label of being poor.

Work, shoddy - poor, work. These are the things that fill their lives.
Only those who have failed to use their childhood knowledge without updating their professional experience to the present are living in a poor state of mind.
The poor and workers find it very difficult to take technical psychology skill development advice. The result is a series of failures in quality of life, career, and business. The rich prioritize their knowledge and seek the advice of experts in their field.

Psychological skill development knowledge counselling and action counselling are very much needed to supplement knowledge, update notification. Those who understand this are gaining access to corporate psychological practice, which can be called corporate psychology, through experts.

The expectation of the poor is that someone should come from somewhere to solve their problem. When that problem is solved, the visitor should run away and disappear. Then they catch his eye, but they do not want to pay him the respect he deserves.

But when it comes to the problem, they immediately meet the person who can solve the problem and solve the problem. Then once the problem is solved, the problem is not found until it is solved. They do not understand the mental state of a person with a psychological disorder who can only be approached for a problem.

Poor mindset runs towards money. In the rich mentality, money runs towards the rich. Underlying the wealthy philosophy and the flawed philosophy is the psychological component, behaviour and function.

Money is energy, and this energy cannot be rented out. But the shape can be changed. The psychological, physiological, sociological function of generating power as alternative energy is how money comes and goes.

https://msklifeclinic.in/corporate-art/

9. THE SECRET OF THE SUCCESS OF CORPORATE PEOPLE

What is the meaning of the word corporate?

Well, we say corporate, corporate. What does the word corporate mean? Corporate is not the name for the activities that give a country or a country economy, as you think!

The so-called corporate is the federation! The corporate company contains the process person can run the company together and distribute the products of that company to the people. People work in that company and thereby meet the needs of the people and grow his own company!

If you clearly understand the true meaning of the word corporate, then you can very easily understand the secret to their series of successes that we are going to tell you next!

Well, what is the difference between a platform business and a corporate business? The process in the platform business is to buy the product and sell it at a high profit - that all! But how do you get that stuff out to people? Ordinary people do not know and do not understand the process by which they are taken to which places by whom! But corporate eyes do not ignore these!

9.1 The Secret to Corporate Success!

Corporate bosses will not always be confused that they know everything! They will be apparent that they know nothing! Because as far as corporate bosses are concerned, business is not an act, that is a process. It is also a Long Term Process with its unique structure and size, including the planning system and auditing system that can execute it !! That is why those who are the managing director of corporate companies do not interfere in any activities! They will leave only to be told who to keep and what actions to complete.

The only knowledge they have knowledge that uses intellectuals!

Yes!!! This concept is the secret of the success of corporate company bosses!

Because once you start a business, it requires continuous monitoring and research progress! This smart work is not something that can be done by an individual with only experience and money !!

9.2 Do you know what to do if you start a business?

There are many rewards to starting a business! They have to keep going one after the other!

1. Start-up strategy
2. Branding, Developing & Promotion
3. Business Management
4. Business Operation & Organizational behaviour
5. Business workspace & Working Environment
6. Financial Debt & Credit Advisory Consulting
7. Human Performance & Development
8. Customer care & Relationship
9. Traditional & Neuro Marketing
10. Business Crisis & Solutions
11. Deconflicting & Dispensing Consultation

All of the functions for such operations must be monitored continuously professionally for all types of business! Starting a business is not as profitable as starting a motor and getting water! If the engine is always running, it is likely to run out of water due to its continuous operation! Not only this, with the help of fire you can do welding!

Similarly, in business, you can't pour debt and make a profit! That requires continuous monitoring and research progress! Knowing this well, corporate bosses can hire professional consultants in all the functions of the business without bumping into themselves and thereby get all the work done efficiently!

But ordinary people who think that they can make a profit by doing business as they know how with money and experience are suffering from different mentalities! This mindset is not giving healthy growth!

TYPES OF PROFESSIONAL CONSULTING

BUSINESS PLANNING & RESOURCE, OUTSOURCING, PROPORTIONAL CONSULTING, STRATEGY CONSULTING, MANAGEMENT & BUSINESS INTELLIGENCE, ORGANIZATIONAL BEHAVIOR CONSULTANCY, WORKPLACE WELLNESS, WORK ENVIRONMENTAL CONSULTANCY, PERFORMANCE AUDITING, BUSINESS FITNESS, BUSINESS DEVELOPMENT PROCESS, BUSINESS DEVELOPMENT & SEGMENT TARGET, FINANCIAL DEBT – CREDIT ADVISORY, HUMAN PERFORMANCE DEVELOPMENT, HUMAN CAPITAL, CUSTOMER CARE & RELATIONSHIP, NEURO MARKETING, TRADITIONAL MARKETING, BUSINESS CRISES & SOLUTIONS.

10. WHO IS PROFESSIONAL CONSULTANT FOR BUSINESS?

Professional consulting is a practice gaining knowledge from experts in the field, rather than trying fixing problems in the business with only our experiential understanding, when there is a lack of knowledge about the industry, such as borrowing money when there is a shortage of money in the business!

We cannot cut our hair ourselves! It requires a proper professional! That means you need a man who knows about it to grow and fix hair! Similarly, only corporate bosses understand the need for a professional to develop and edit the business! When ordinary people understand that business life is so much higher than hair, their business is sure to succeed!

10.1 The Importance of consulting in business

Corporate employers hire professional consultants to spend millions on a variety of business needs. For example, they are correcting the conflicts between the internal customer and those who can work, correcting their stress, reducing the conflict between the external customer and the business, reducing their stress and developing their business, regenerating the business loss, and so on.

That why they spearhead many times more profit than they spend! But the primary reason for the failure of ordinary people business is to say that we do not understand all the functions required for business, or do it ourselves without taking any professional consulting!

This concept is precisely how a car buyer can become a car mechanic! If you go to the right mechanic when the problem comes in the car, that problem will be solved! But the car will be ruined by its boss if we try to fix it ourselves! Corporate companies are getting their businesses ready one by one with professional consultants just like they are getting the car ready with the mechanic. Their job is not to get the car ready! But their interest is to travelling in their vehicle.

This mindset is the secret of corporate success! Understand this, and you too, can become a winner! To understand the need for Professional consulting to become a winner!

10.2 Professional Consulting – How it Works?

Let us look at a few examples to understand this! Take the ballpoint pen you use! Look at that tip where it writes! One of the smallest cylinders in it is rolling! That is why the pen writes with ink! Can you guess how many types of professional consultancy have worked to design this?

When building a house, can you imagine how many different technologies and safety features are used in the materials used in it and its design? Can you understand how many types of professional consultants knowledge technology is behind this?

You note a lending bank or lending company. How many types of documents are being checked for lending to you, and at what level? Have you ever noticed how many different techniques are used when lending and collecting a debt? Do you know how many types of professional consulting people are behind these activities?

Take movie or TV serials. It is different to act in a film; it is different from creating a story, it is different from telling the information to the producer and the approval bank to select the technicians to make the film and run it to finish the movie! Do you know how many hundreds of Professional consulting people are behind each of these types of activities? Why so much? Only the salary paid to those who design a poster for a film will make you understand the importance of this field!

There are millions of businesses using professional consulting people. If you think that 'I know everything' will become the No.1 business that bumps into you, you should go back about 200 years and do business because there were very few business investments during that period!

Take a jewellery ad! There will be at least 100 Professional consulting people behind that ad! None of these people come up with ads! It is not visible outside! Even if you search for their office, there is not even a board about them! The reason is that just as the Rolls-Royce car does not need advertising, so those who see the advertisement do not know consulting people's beauty and do not know how to use them. Only corporate bosses will come looking for them! His is because they only have the knowledge to use these geniuses!

10.3 How to take consulting?

If that is the practice in most companies today, call a trainer for something. He will come and put some PowerPoint on the slide for those who work in that company and leave! Expect business to grow right away. But there is no chance of that happening!

Professional consulting is not training and learning! This consultation is not a one day, two-day workshop! Stay tuned with the consultant for what you want to achieve with your growth through 'Mind Partnership'! He would have joined you too!\

Many people who consult for business development are those who leave the book or existing business theories behind. But only a handful of professional consulting firms create their ideas based on their many years of research and develop many winners and act as mind partners for many corporate companies. Notable company in that category is Business Branding Consultancy (BBC)! The BBC is based on the theory of 'Mind-Set Knowledge (MSK)'!

10.4 Business Branding Consultancy (BBC)

They see the world according to how the Mind Set of every human being is. The reason that the world succeeds or fails is because of the way they see and approach that world! This concept is the basis for MSK theory!

MSK Muhaiyuddin discovered this Mind Set Knowledge based on about 25 years of research! Muhaiyuddin then founded the MSK Life Clinic Foundation in Coimbatore, Tamilnadu, India! This clinic is the first Life Clinic started in South India!

To Know about MSK Muhaiyuddin visit: https://msklifeclinic.in/ Here they create a Mind Lab and measure the people who seek them in four parameters! That is, *(1)* education, *(2)* economics, *(3)* psychological health, and *(4)* social well-being. What a man lacks in this will destroy the other three things from him!

- This is why even those who have studied big business management, but not doing! They are doing only management work.

- Business owners may have another suspicion. After learning this stuff, our competitors know it too, or they can beat us with it by drinking coffee, of course not!

- Because MSK theory is designed to work individually for you depending on the uniqueness of your work! This uniqueness is the speciality of MSK Theory.

- Even the comments we have made here about business are confirmed based on the MSK Theory! You can find more information about MSK Life Clinic at www.msklifeclinic.in and on the MSK Life TV YouTube channel!

- Launched as part of the MSK Life Clinic, the BBC today has successfully produced many winners and is at the forefront of providing professional consulting to many leading corporates!

- There are so many reasons why we should only mention the BBC here! Especially.

- You can get the right, most accurate and precise advice on the BBC on any problem!

- Those who have joined as Mind Partner here can contact us directly at any time or by phone and ask for solutions!

- BBC consultants will stay with you until you succeed!!

- From this New Year onwards, even those who are unable to come directly have decided to offer telecommunication consulting through a new system called MSK Online Consulting through their smart phone screen!

- For more information about this Business Branding Consultancy, call BBC consultants. You can contact them at +919360053930!

Some Final Words!

- How money works depends on how his mind works!

- How to get money is different; how to make money is different!

- You can shorten the time by putting money! But you can't shrink labour to make money !!

- Business does not need money! The mind needs it!

- We are giving interest to the bank only because we have no interest in knowing how to do business! If we have the excellent wish in industry, we can put money in the bank and buy a stake from them!

- Business intelligence is a process that starts with data integration, collects information and makes it intelligent until Decision Making!

- Only those who know to use intellectuals are promoted to become corporate businessmen! This mindset is the secret of their business success.

- Mind partnership is something that can develop the business with you! The company has been doing this successfully for about 25 years personally Business Branding Consultancy (Web:https://msklifeclinic.in/ and Tel: +919360053930 for details)

Congratulations on touching the peak in the right way and the honourable profession!

ABOUT THE AUTHOR

MSK Muhaiyuddin, Psychologist,

Founder & CEO,

MSK Life Clinic Foundation

Mr.Muhaiyuddin is popularly known as MSK, because MSK @ Mind Set Knowledge is world's first theoretical invention about human life system. Invention becomes, initial to the name. Now, Mind Set Knowledge Muhaiyuddin @ MSK Muhaiyuddin researches on the area of Human working memory in relation to abilities and fluid crystallized intelligence and occupational stress and job satisfaction among corporate professionals International certified six sigma consultant and International soft skill trainer (UK) .

MSK Muhaiyuddin passion for human life improvement is inspired him to start clinic for life collaborating with his own MSK formula (Mind Set Knowledge). MSK Life Clinic is India's first clinic to improve to human life without drug by modifying their MIND SET KNOWLEDGE (MSK) to develop the individual's educational, economic, social status and healthy mind, as well as to improve Industrial productivity with mutual profit. MSK Muhaiyuddin research continues in using more minds set reorganizing and knowledge replacing therapeutic learning approaches with more humanistic nurturing nature.

You can get more details about MSK in www.msklifeclinic.in

www.ingramcontent.com/pod-product-compliance
Lightning Source LLC
Chambersburg PA
CBHW070856220526
45466CB00005B/2016